Grammar Works
Answer Key

1

Mick Gammidge

CAMBRIDGE
UNIVERSITY PRESS

PUBLISHED BY THE PRESS SYNDICATE OF THE UNIVERSITY OF CAMBRIDGE
The Pitt Building, Trumpington Street, Cambridge, United Kingdom

CAMBRIDGE UNIVERSITY PRESS
The Edinburgh Building, Cambridge CB2 2RU, UK   http://www.cup.cam.ac.uk
40 West 20th Street, New York, NY 10011–4211, USA   http://www.cup.org
10 Stamford Road, Oakleigh, Melbourne 3166, Australia
Ruiz de Alarcón 13, 28014 Madrid, Spain

First published 2000

Printed in Great Britain at J W Arrowsmith Ltd, Bristol

ISBN 0 521 79762 4 Answer Key 1
ISBN 0 521 55542 6 Student's Book 1

Student's Book answers

1 Hello. You're new here

1b 1 I
2 you
3 *she*
4 he
5 it
6 we
7 you
8 they
9 they
10 they

2 I am = I'm
you are = you're
he is = he's
she is = she's
it is = it's
we are = *we're*
you are = you're
they are = they're

3 1 *I'm*
2 She
3 You
4 They're
5 We
6 It's

4a 's not   're not
4b I: 'm not, *am not*
she, he, it: 's not, isn't, is not
we, you, they: aren't, 're not, are not

5 1 ✗
2 ✗
3 ✗
4 ✗
5 ✔
6 ✗
7 ✗

6 1 *It isn't fast. It's slow.*
2 *He's happy.*
3 They aren't old. They're young.
4 They're hot.
6 She's tired.
7 They're busy.

7 Answers will vary.

Puzzle
Eric is right. (If Linda is right, then Mark is also right in saying Eric is wrong. But only one person is right, so it must be Eric.)

2 Who are you?

1b Are you OK?
Who is she?

2
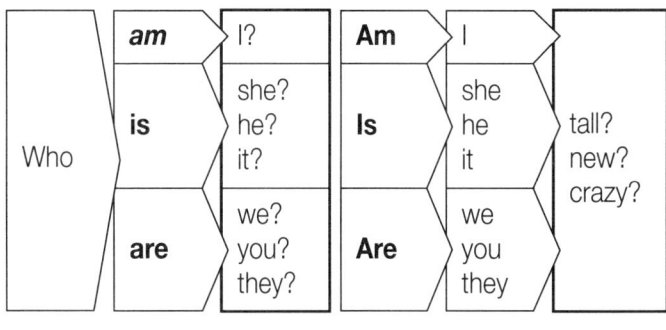

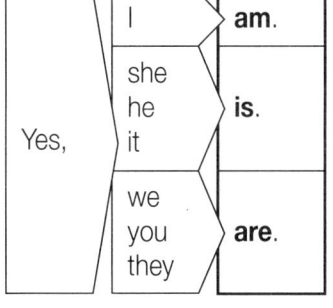 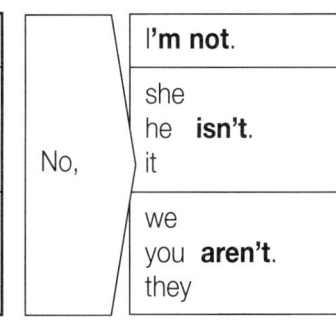

3 1 *Is Lion Boy strong?*
2 Is Spider Boy crazy?
3 Is Cat Girl brave?
4 Are Spider Boy and Cat Girl old?
5 Are Lion Boy and Spider Boy clever?
6 Is Cat Girl stupid?

4 1 *Yes, he is.*
2 No, he isn't.
3 Yes, she is.
4 No, they aren't.
5 Yes, they are.
6 No, she isn't.

5 1 *Who is he?   He's Batman.*
2 Who are they?   They're Oasis.
3 Who is she?   She's Cleopatra.
4 Who are they?   They're Tom and Jerry.
5 Who is he?   He's Tiger Woods.
6 Who is she?   She's Björk.

6 1 I'm
2 Who
3 you
4 I'm
5 You're
6 who's

7 Answers will vary.

Puzzle
1 21 (the number 3 is added to the previous number in the sequence)
2 12 (the number 2, then 3, then 4, is added to the previous number in the box)
3 25 (the numbers in the boxes are the squares of 2, 3, 4 and 5)

3 A star prize! What is it?

1b 1 What is it?
2 What are they?
1c 1 (It's) a car.
2 (They're) a computer, an exercise bike (and) a television(.)
1d What is it?

2b dishes, babies, bags, cakes

3

s	es	ies	irregular
zoos	*glasses*	parties	teeth
elephants	foxes	cities	sheep

4a a camera   an exercise bike   a television   an alarm clock

5 1 *It's a glass*.
2 It's an exercise bike.
3 It's a party.
4 It's an alarm clock.
5 It's an ice cream.
6 It's a cake.

6 1 *What are they?*   *They're sheep.*
2 What are they?   They're foxes.
3 What are they?   They're wolves.
4 What is it?   It's a lion.
5 What is it?   It's an elephant.
6 What is it?   It's a mouse.

7 Answers will vary.

Puzzle
Possible words: bag(s), bike(s), cake(s), camera(s), mice, match(es), dish, city, cities, party, parties, sheep, watch(es)

4 It's an excellent film!

1 **** = excellent

2a 1 It's an excellent film.
2 It's a great adventure.
2b They're great actors.
2d 1 She's **a** good actor.
2 He's **a** funny man.
3 It's **an** exciting adventure.

2e For adjective + noun, look at the first letter of the adjective. Use *an* with vowels (a, e, i, o, u) and use *a* with consonants.

3 1 *He's a tall man.*
2 It's an exciting film.
3 He's a young boy/child.
4 It's an expensive computer.
5 She's a short woman.
6 He's an old man.

4a *Batman Forever* is (1) **an** excellent film! (2) **The** film's exciting.
4b *Batman Forever* is (1) **a** great adventure. (2) **The** adventure is exciting.
4c The first time a singular noun is introduced, use *a/an*. The second time and after, use *the* for singular nouns and plural nouns.

5 1 *The man is 2 metres.*
2 The film is great.
3 The boy/child is 2.
4 The computer is $100,000.
5 The woman is 1.25 metres.
6 The man is 99.

6 1 *She isn't an untidy person. She's tidy.*
2 She isn't a sad person. She's happy.
3 She isn't a serious person. She's funny.
4 She isn't an unfriendly person. She's friendly.
5 She isn't a lazy person. She's hardworking.

7 Answers will vary.

Puzzle
a **c**lever **c**at – the first letter of the adjective and the first letter of the noun are the same.

5 These are my posters

1b 1 B
2 C
3 A

2 he – his;   they – their;   it – its;   she – her;   *Kylie – Kylie's*

3 1 *His name is Wallace.*
2 Its name is Gromit.
3 Her name is Kylie.
4 Their names are Wallace and Gromit.
5 My name is Paulo.
6 Our names are Paulo and Carlos.

4 1 *It's Hank's telescope. It's his telescope.*
2 It's Dollar's chair. It's its chair.
3 It's Hank's boat. It's his boat.
4 They're Betty's CDs. They're her CDs.
5 It's Hank's desk. It's his desk.
6 It's Dollar's bed. It's its bed.

5

	near	far	1	2+
this	✔	✘	✔	✘
these	✔	✘	✘	✔
that	✘	✔	✔	✘
those	✘	✔	✘	✔

6 1 *This is my dog.* Those are my sheep.
   2 That's my dog. Those are my sheep.
   3 That's my dog. These are my sheep.
   4 This is my dog. These are my sheep.

7 Answers will vary.

Puzzle
Tom (Tom's mother's only brother's only sister = Tom's mother; so
Tom's mother's only child = Tom.)

6 Whose breakfast is this?

1b 1 Babs
   2 Clare
   3 Al
   4 Dave

2 *It's my breakfast.*   *It's mine.*
   It's your breakfast.   It's yours.
   It's his breakfast.   It's his.
   It's her breakfast.   It's hers.
   It's our breakfast.   It's ours.
   It's their breakfast.   It's theirs.
   It's Dave's breakfast.   It's Dave's.
   It's the dog's breakfast. It's the dog's.
   It's the dogs' breakfast. It's the dogs'.

3 1 mine
   2 ours
   3 theirs
   4 yours
   5 hers
   6 his

4a 1 Whose breakfast is this?
    2 Is this yours?
4b 1 Whose breakfasts are those?
    2 Are those yours?

5 1 *Whose shirt is this?*
   2 Whose socks are these?
   3 Is this yours?
   4 Are these yours?
   5 Whose shoe is this?

6 1 is mine
   2 are hers
   3 is theirs
   4 is his

7 Answers will vary.

Puzzle
A = fish   B = bike   C = bag   D = shoe

Check point 1–6

1 1 *It's old and it's dirty. What is it?*
   2 They're fast and they're dangerous. What are they?
   3 It's strong and it's slow. What is it?
   4 He's short and he's happy. Who is he?
   5 She's tall and she's sad. Who is she?

2 1 *It's a car.*
   2 They're leopards.
   3 It's an elephant.
   4 He's Bill.
   5 She's Ann.

3 1 *Are they young?*   Yes, they are.
   2 Are they friendly?   Yes, they are.
   3 Are they beautiful?   Yes, they are.
   4 Are they clever?   No, they aren't!
   5 Is it new?   No, it isn't.
   6 Is it red?   No, it isn't.
   7 Is it fast?   Yes, it is.
   8 Is it expensive?   Er, yes, it is!

4a 1 *It's an expensive bike.*
    2 It's a funny comic.
    3 It's an old university.
    4 He's an untidy boy.
    5 It's an exciting film.
    6 It's a lazy cat.
4b 1 *The bike is expensive.*
    2 The comic is funny.
    3 The university is old.
    4 The boy is untidy.
    5 The film is exciting.
    6 The cat is lazy.

5

I	my	*mine*
you	your	yours
he	his	his
she	her	hers
it	its	~~its~~
Sue	Sue's	Sue's
the cat	the cat's	the cat's
we	our	ours
you	your	yours
they	their	theirs
the cats	the cats'	the cats'

6 1 Whose mouse is this?
    That's mine.
   2 Whose burger/sandwich is this?
    That's hers.
   3 Whose socks are these?
    Those are his.

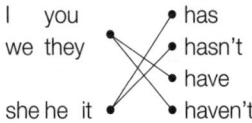

Tina hasn't got a home

1b 1 Yes, she is.
2 No, they aren't.

2a

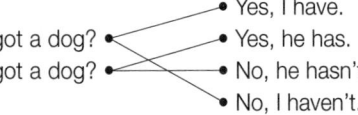

2b ? Has she got a home?
+ She has got a home.
– She hasn't got a home.

2c

Have you got a dog? → Yes, I have.
Has he got a dog? → Yes, he has.
→ No, he hasn't.
→ No, I haven't.

3 1 *Joe has got a flat.*
2 Joe hasn't got a garden.
3 Joe has got a cat.
4 Mr and Mrs Mill have got a house.
5 Mr and Mrs Mill have got a daughter.
6 Mr and Mrs Mill have got a mouse.

4 1 *I've got a toothache.*
2 You've got a bad tooth.
3 He's got a sore finger.
4 They've got broken legs.
5 I've got a headache.
6 She's got a stomach-ache.

5 1 *Has your school got a computer?*
2 Have you got a computer (at home)?
3 Has your father got a computer (at work)?
4 Has your mother got a computer (at work)?
5 Have your grandparents got a computer?

6 Answers will vary.

7 Answers will vary.

Puzzle
Anne = 2, Bill = 3, Clare = 1; altogether = 6

Are there any comics?

1b a ✔ b ✘ c ✘

2

	+	–	?
singular (1)	*a/an*	a/an	a/an
plural (2+)	some	any	any

3

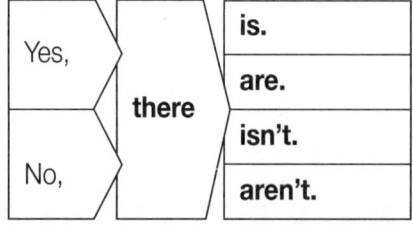

4 1 *There is a box.*
2 There isn't a ball.
3 There isn't a bike.
4 There aren't any books.
5 There is an axe.
6 There are some cassettes.
7 There are some magazines.
8 There aren't any skates.

5 1 *There is a swimming pool.*
2 There are some telephones.
3 There is a car park.
4 There are some shops.
5 There is a restaurant.
6 There is a garden.
7 There are some lifts.

6a 1 *Is there a swimming pool?*
2 Are there any telephones?
3 Is there a car park?
4 Are there any shops?
5 Is there a restaurant?
6 Is there a garden?
7 Are there any lifts?

6b 1 *No, there isn't.*
2 Yes, there are.
3 Yes, there is.
4 No, there aren't.
5 Yes, there is.
6 No, there isn't.
7 Yes, there are.

7 Answers will vary.

Puzzle
The black squares are A2, C2, B4 and C4.

9 How much orange juice is there?

1b 1 *50 grams*
  2 1 litre
  3 34
  4 3

2a 1 are
  2 many, are
  3 is
  4 much, is

2b much – sugar, orange juice
  many – oranges, glasses

3

ORANGES – Countable nouns		SUGAR – Uncountable nouns	
bananas	eggs	cereal	meat
burgers	sandwiches	coffee	oil
cakes	sausages	lemonade	water

4 1 There are some biscuits.
  2 *There is some chicken.*
  3 There is some coffee.
  4 There are some sausages.
  5 There are some sandwiches.
  6 There are some bananas.
  7 There is some meat.
  8 There is some lemonade.

5 1 How many biscuits are there?
  2 *How much chicken is there?*
  3 How much coffee is there?
  4 How many sausages are there?
  5 How many sandwiches are there?
  6 How many bananas are there?
  7 How much meat is there?
  8 How much lemonade is there?

6 1 *any*
  2 there
  3 much
  4 some
  5 many
  6 are
  7 are
  8 is
  9 isn't

7 Answers will vary.

Puzzle
Five: there are only two brothers altogether.

10 What's in your fridge?

1b 1 It's *in* the sink.
  2 It's under the table.
  3 They're on the table.

2

 on
 in
 under

 behind
between
 *above*

 next to/*by/beside*
 in front of

3 1 *Where is the dog?*
  2 Where is the newspaper?
  3 Where are the keys?
  4 Where is the clock?
  5 Where are the books?

4 1 next to
  2 on
  3 in
  4 between
  5 in front of

5 1 *There is a fish next to* some lemonade.
  2 There is some lemonade between a fish and some orange juice.
  3 There is some meat above some sausages.
  4 There is some chicken behind some eggs.
  5 There are some eggs in front of some chicken.
  6 There are some sausages under some meat.

6 1 *The fish is between the* lemonade and the orange juice.
  2 The lemonade is next to the fish.
  3 The meat is under the sausages.
  4 The chicken is behind the ice cream.
  5 The eggs are above the chicken.
  6 The sausages are next to the eggs.

7 Answers will vary.

Puzzle
There are three ducks. Two ducks are in front of the last duck; two ducks are behind the first duck and the second duck is between the first and the last duck.

11 Don't sit in the sun

1b 1 ✔ 2 ✘ 3 ✔ 4 ✘ 5 ✔
1c don't

2 1 **Drink** lemonade.
  2 **Don't** stand in the sun at midday.

3 1 d
  2 c
  3 a
  4 e
  5 b

4 1 *Don't take photos.*
  2 Turn left.
  3 Don't drop litter.
  4 Wash your hands.
  5 Don't walk on the grass.
  6 Don't turn right.
  7 Don't drink the water.

5 Dos: 1 *Do* 2 Wear 3 Listen 4 Be
  Don'ts: 1 Don't eat 2 Don't play 3 Don't sit 4 Don't run

6 1 *Wash your hands.*
  2 Don't stand on the/your chairs.
  3 Use a ruler.
  4 Put litter in the bin.
  5 Don't run.

7 Answers will vary.

Puzzle

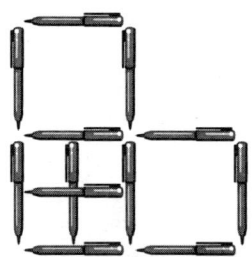

12 What can you do?

1b 1 ✔ 2 ✘ 3 ✔
1c Yes, they can.

2 **What can** they do?
  They **can** crawl. They **can't** walk.
  Can they run?
  No, they **can't**.

3 1 *Children can read. Gorillas can't read.*
  2 Children can write. Gorillas can't write.
  3 Children can climb trees. Gorillas can climb trees.
  4 Children can run. Gorillas can run.
  5 Children can use a telephone. Gorillas can't use a telephone.

4 1 *Can he speak Chinese?*
  2 Can he swim?
  3 Can they play tennis?
  4 Can she sing?
  5 Can she ride a bike?
  6 Can they dance?

5 1 *No, he can't.*
  2 No, he can't.
  3 Yes, they can.
  4 Yes, she can.
  5 No, she can't.
  6 Yes, they can.

6 **What can** you *see*? **Can** you **see** Saturn?
  No, I **can't. I can't see** Saturn. **I can see** the back of your head!

7 Answers will vary.

Puzzle
an old woman and a young woman; a rabbit and a bird

Check point 7–12

1a 1 *Have you got any books in your bag?*
  2 Have you got an apple (in your bag)?
  3 Have you got a dictionary (in your bag)?
  4 Have you got any sandwiches (in your bag)?
1b 1–4 Yes, I have. / No, I haven't. Answers will vary.

2a 1 *Are there any* parks?
  2 Is there a post office?
  3 Are there any shops?
  4 Is there a swimming pool?
  5 Is there a bank?
  6 Are there any restaurants?
2b 1 Yes, there are.
  2 No, there isn't.
  3 Yes, there are.
  4 Yes, there is.
  5 No, there isn't.
  6 No, there aren't.

3 1 *How much lemonade is there?*
  2 How much ice cream is there?
  3 How much chicken is there?
  4 How many glasses are there?
  5 How many sausages are there?
  6 How many cakes are there?
  7 How much orange juice is there?

4 1 *Where's the orange juice?*
    It's in front of the lemonade.
  2 Where are the glasses?
    They're next to the chicken.
  3 Where's the chicken?
    It's between the glasses and the cakes.
  4 Where are the sandwiches?
    They're on the small table.

5 Where are the sausages?
    They're in front of the ice cream.
6 Where's the lemonade?
    It's behind the orange juice.

5 1 *Don't climb* the tree.
    2 Don't eat it!
    3 Wash your hands.
    4 Read your book.
    5 Don't sit on the cat!

6 1 *Can she swim?   Yes, she can.*
    2 Can they climb trees?   Yes, they can.
    3 Can he read?   No, he can't.
    4 Can she draw/write?   No, she can't.
    5 Can they sing?   Yes, they can.
    6 Can they play computer games?   Yes, they can.

13 Papuans live in the Pacific

1b 1 C ✗
2 A ✔
3 B ✗

2a + They **live** in villages.
– They **don't live** in cities.
2b + They **wear** necklaces.
– They **don't wear** school uniforms.

3 1 *Papuans don't eat hamburgers.*
2 Americans like baseball.
3 Canadians don't grow bananas.
4 Italians eat pizzas.
5 Brazilians grow coffee.
6 Papuans don't speak Italian.

4 1 eat, drink
2 don't go, listen
3 don't live, live
4 live, don't drive, ride

5 1 *Mosquitoes don't eat chips. They drink blood.*
2 Cowboys don't drive buses. They ride horses.
3 Fish don't fly in the sky. They swim in the sea.
4 I don't speak a Papuan language. I speak …

6 1 collect stamps   2 make models   3 play football
4 read comics   5 ride a motorbike   6 watch TV

7 Answers will vary.

Puzzle
'Babs and I don't play a musical instrument' is the key information and where to start. The rest is elimination.

Al – drums; Clare – guitar; Dave – stamps; Babs – models

14 Do you play the drums?

1b ☐3 ☐1 ☐2

2a 1 Yes, I do.
2 I go to school in London.
3 I go to school in the morning.
4 I walk to school.
5 I study science.
2b 1 **Do** you get up at 7.00?   No, I **don't**.
2 **When do** you get up?   I **get up** at 6.00.

3 1 *Do you* drive a car?
2 Do you listen to the radio?
3 Do you study English?
4 Do you do (your) homework?
5 Do you sing songs?
6 Do you play the piano?

4 Yes, I do. / No, I don't. Answers will vary.

5a in – the morning   on – Monday   at – 1.00/2.00
5b 1 *at*
2 at
3 at
4 in
5 in
6 At
7 On
8 in
9 in

6 1 *Where do you go to school?*
2 When do you start class?
3 How do you go to school?
4 What do you study?
5 Do you have tests?
6 When do you do your homework?
7 Do you like homework?

7 Answers will vary.

Puzzle
They sing songs.
The first letter of the verb is the same as the first letter of the day!

15 Sometimes he doesn't wake up for school

1c 1 takes
2 doesn't

2b watches   tidies   reads   does

3 1 *She doesn't eat vegetables. She eats burgers.*
2 She doesn't read newspapers. She reads comics.
3 She studies English. She doesn't study Chinese.
4 She doesn't watch football on TV. She watches music.

4 1 *Does she eat burgers?   Yes, she does.*
2 Does she read comics?   Yes, she does.
3 Does she study Chinese?   No, she doesn't.
4 Does she watch football?   No, she doesn't.

5 100% always   sometimes   0% never

6 1 *She sometimes goes to the cinema.*
2 She often meets her friends.
3 She never goes jogging.
4 She rarely tidies her bedroom.
5 She usually listens to the radio.
6 She always brushes her teeth.

7 Answers will vary.

Puzzle
80 minutes = 1 hour and 20 minutes; so the journey takes the same time in both cars!

16 She hates speaking English

1b 1 ✗ 2 ✔ 3 ✗ 4 ✔ 5 ✗

2b she – her   he – him   it – it   they – them

3 1 them
2 us
3 you
4 her
5 them
6 it, me

4a dancing – dance   lying – lie   swimming – swim   singing – sing

4b Words ending in:
- -e: -~~e~~ + -ing
- -ie: -~~ie~~ + -y + -ing
- a vowel and then a consonant, (e.g. -ut, -un, -it), double – × 2
  – the consonant + -ing
  - Other words: + -ing

4c speak – *speaking*   take – taking   die – dying   run – running
wash – washing   make – making   tie – tying   put – putting

5 1 *He hates getting up.*
2 She hates using the computer.
3 They enjoy/like/love walking.
4 She enjoys/likes/loves shopping.
5 They enjoy/like/love eating.
6 He enjoys/likes/loves lying in bed.

6 1 *them*
2 her
3 studying
4 writing
5 me
6 reading
7 us
8 you

7 Answers will vary.

Puzzle
The professor loves verbs with **an** in them!

17 They're standing up and shouting

1b 1 B
2 D
3 A
4 C

2 1 *Are*, playing   2 *Is*, isn't, She's listening   3 Are, are

3 1 *I'm painting* a picture.
2 You're sitting on my coat.
3 You aren't wearing your school uniform.
4 Look! He's walking.
5 You aren't doing your homework.
6 They aren't eating their dinner.

4 1 *She's dancing.*
2 She's writing on the board.
3 They're drawing.
4 He's playing a computer game.
5 They're reading a comic.

5 1 *Are you dancing?*
No, I'm not. I'm tidying the books.
2 Are you writing on the board?
No, I'm not. I'm cleaning it.
3 Are you drawing?
No, we're not. We're writing.
4 Are you playing a computer game?
No, I'm not. I'm using a calculator.
5 Are you reading a comic?
No, we're not. We're studying.

6 1 'm telephoning
2 's riding
3 's wearing
4 's carrying
5 's
6 aren't listening

7 Answers will vary.

Puzzle
670 books – 7% of students have one book, half the remainder have two books and the other half have no books – which equals one book for each student.

18 What is James doing?

1b 1 looks   2 is looking
1c looks   is looking

2a 1 What is James doing?
2 Where is James sitting?
2b 1 He's looking at the moon.
2 He's sitting in his bedroom.

3b

present simple	present continuous
I study	I'm studying
you study	you're studying
she studies	she's studying
he studies	he's studying
it studies	it's studying
we study	we're studying
they study	they're studying

4
1 *likes*
2 isn't listening
3 is thinking
4 knows
5 watches
6 knows
7 does ... know
8 is sleeping

5
1 What are you doing?
2 I'm cooking.
3 What are you cooking?
4 What do you want?
5 Where are your cassettes?
6 Where are you going?

6
1 *What are you doing?* I'm looking at his teeth.
   What do you do? *I'm a dentist.*
2 What do you do? I'm a doctor.
   What are you doing? I'm looking at your eyes.
3 What are you doing? I'm brushing the horse.
   What do you do? I'm a farmer.

7 Answers will vary.

Puzzle
His son.

Check point 13 – 18

1
1 studies ... on
2 eats ... in
3 studies ... on ... at
4 plays ... on ... in
5 studies ... at ... on

2
1 *always wins*
2 rarely win
3 often wins
4 usually win
5 sometimes wins
6 never wins

3
1 **When do** we **sleep**? At night.
2 **Where do** we **buy** magazines? At a newsagent.
3 **What do** English people **eat** for breakfast? Bacon and eggs, toast or cereal.
4 **How do** we **learn** new words? We use a dictionary.
5 **Where do** gorillas **live**? In Africa.
6 **When do** we **get up**? In the morning.

4

1	I	my	*mine*	me
2	you	your	yours	you
3	she	her	hers	her
4	he	his	his	him
5	it	~~its~~	its	it
6	Kim	Kim's	Kim's	*Kim*
7	the cat	the cat's	the cat's	*the cat*
8	we	our	*ours*	us
9	they	*their*	theirs	them
10	the cats	the cats'	the cats'	*the cats*

5 Answers will vary.
1 I like, hate, etc. ... / don't like playing football.
2 I _____ eating sweets.
3 My friend _____s / doesn't like studying maths.
4 My mother _____s / doesn't like washing the dishes.
5 I _____ / don't like tidying my bedroom.
6 My teacher _____s / doesn't like speaking English.
7 I _____ / don't like sitting in the sun.
8 My grandparents _____ / don't like watching TV.
9 My father _____s / doesn't like going to work.

6
1 *What are they doing?* *They're dancing.*
2 What is it doing? It's sleeping.
3 What is he doing? He's getting up.
4 What is she doing? She's reading (a magazine).
5 What are they doing? They're playing football.
6 What is she doing? She's eating (an ice cream).
7 What are they doing? They're listening to the radio.

19 You're going to be busy!

1b future

2a 1 is going to come
   2 aren't going to have

2b 1 You aren't going to have any free time.
   2 You're going to be busy.
   3 You are going to have a good week.
   4 You aren't going to have a bad week.

3 1 *Paulo's dad is going to open the window.*
   2 The cat is going to jump on the table.
   3 Paulo's brother/Carlos is going to kick the cat.
   4 Paulo's sister is going to eat some/the chocolates.
   5 Paulo's mum is going to answer the phone.
   6 Paulo is going to go out.

4 1 *She's going to throw the ball.*
   2 He's going to catch the ball.
   3 They're going to drop the plates.
   4 It's going to break.
   5 They're going to fall in the river.

5 1 *They aren't going to come.*
   2 He isn't going to ride his bike/it.
   3 He isn't going to get up.
   4 She isn't going to eat (the) sausages/them.
   5 They aren't going to do their homework.

6 1 *He's going to wash his dog on Saturday.*
   2 He's going to take his bike to the bike shop on Saturday.
   3 He's going to write to his grandma on Sunday.
   4 He's going to meet Sue on Sunday.
   5 He's going to do his music project on Sunday.

7 Answers will vary.

Puzzle
Yes – it's this boy's party, or his brother's.

20 What are you going to watch?

1b Nature Watch   The Thing 3

2a 1 Is he going to watch TV?
   2 Are they going to watch TV?

2b
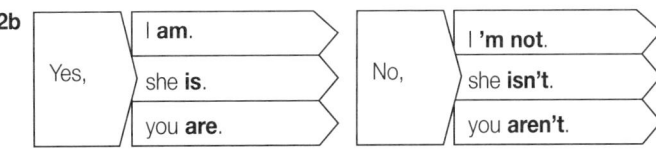

Yes,	I **am**.	No,	I **'m not**.
	she **is**.		she **isn't**.
	you **are**.		you **aren't**.

3 1 *d* 2 e 3 a 4 b 5 c
   1 *Are they going to* watch Nature Watch?
   2 Is he going to do his homework?
   3 Is she going to go to the party?
   4 Are they going to do any sport next weekend?
   5 Are you going to fly to Turkey?

4 1 *It's going to be cloudy in the east.*
   2 It's going to rain in the west.
   3 It's going to snow in the north.
   4 It's going to be sunny in the south.

5 1 *Is it going to be cloudy in the east?*
     No, it isn't. It's going to be sunny.
   2 Is it going to rain in the west?
     No, it isn't. It's going to be cloudy.
   3 Is it going to snow in the north?
     No, it isn't. It's going to rain.
   4 Is it going to be sunny in the south?
     Yes, it is.

6 1 Where are you going to go?
   2 When are you going to go?
   3 Who are you going to go with?
   4 What are you going to do?

7 Answers will vary.

Puzzle

21 Who were they?

1b past

2a is – was   isn't – wasn't   are – were   aren't – weren't

2b 1 Where were they from?
   2 They were from Africa.
   3 Were they tall?
   4 No, they weren't.

3 1 *She was*
   2 It was
   3 She wasn't
   4 There weren't
   5 She was

4 1 *Was it*
   2 Was it
   3 Was it
   4 Were they
   5 Were they
   6 Were

5
1 *Yes, it was.*
2 Yes, it was.
3 No, it wasn't.
4 No, they weren't.
5 Yes, they were.
6 Yes, they were.

6a
1 *What was the Colossus?*
2 Who was Cleopatra?
3 What was the Titanic?
4 Who were the Wright brothers?
5 Who was Martin Luther King?
6 What were the Hanging Gardens?
7 Who was Amelia Earhart?

6b
1 The Colossus: see exercises 4 and 5.
2 Cleopatra was a queen of Ancient Egypt at the time of Julius Caesar.
3 The Titanic hit an iceberg on its first voyage across the Atlantic in April 1912. The ship sank and 1,513 people died.
4 The Wright brothers (Wilbur and Orville) flew the first aeroplane in December 1903.
5 Martin Luther King was an American black civil rights leader. He died in 1968.
6 The Hanging Gardens: see exercises 4 and 5.
7 Amelia Earhart was, in 1928, the first woman to fly across the Atlantic. Her plane disappeared over the Pacific in 1937.

7 Answers will vary.

Puzzle
1st = Number 2; 2nd = Number 7; 3rd = Number 18;
4th = Number 9

22 They invented printing

1b 1 ✓ 2 ✗ 3 ✗

2a past
2b do – did don't – didn't does – did doesn't – didn't
2c 1 stopped 2 didn't stop 3 visited 4 didn't visit

3a start**ed** stop**ped** stud**ied** like**d**
3b carried loved wanted stirred

4 1 *painted* 2 studied 3 sailed 4 played

5
1 *They didn't study English. They studied science.*
2 They listened to music. They didn't listen to the radio.
3 They lived in Asia. They didn't live in America.
4 They visited Africa. They didn't visit Europe.
5 They cooked rice. They didn't cook burgers.
6 They invented fireworks. They didn't invent (the) TV.

6
1 lived
2 were
3 studied
4 sailed
5 didn't visit
6 enjoyed

7 invented
8 didn't play

7 Answers will vary.

Puzzle
c walked across the Atacama desert – the first letter of the verb is the same as the first letter of the season.

23 Aunt Flo visited us

1b 1 ✗ 2 ✓ 3 ✗

2
1 had
2 made
3 gave
4 ate
5 sat
6 told
7 sang
8 drank
9 went

3
1 We *went to the zoo.*
2 Carlos rode an elephant.
3 We saw a gorilla.
4 I gave it a banana.
5 It threw the banana.
6 Dad fell down!

4a
1 Did you have a good weekend?   No, I didn't.
2 Did she enjoy the weekend?   Yes, she did.
4b
1 When did she go?
2 Where did they go?
3 What did they see?

5
1 Did the Ancient Chinese eat rice?
  Yes, they did. They didn't eat chips.
2 Did the Ancient Chinese drink tea?
  Yes, they did. They didn't drink coffee.
3 Did dinosaurs have big bodies?
  Yes, they did. They didn't have big brains.
4 Did Attila the Hun ride a motorcycle?
  No, he didn't. He rode a horse.
5 Did Columbus go to Australia?
  No, he didn't. He went to America.

6
1 *Who were these people?*
2 When did they live?
3 Where did they live?
4 What did they eat?
5 What did they make?

7 Answers will vary.

Puzzle
There are three women: a daughter, a mother and a grandmother. The mother is also a daughter, as the grandmother is her mother.

1b 1 ✗   2 ✗   3 ✗

2b 1 c   2 a   3 b

2c Why are they running?

3 1 *Why are you late?*
   2 *Because I missed the bus.*
   3 *Why did you miss the bus?*
   4 *Because I got up late.*
   5 Why did you get up late?
   6 Because I woke up late.
   7 Why did you wake up late?
   8 Because I went to bed late.
   9 Why did you go to bed late?
   10 Because I watched the eclipse last night.

4a 1 d
   2 b
   3 c
   4 a

4b How high is Mount Everest?

4d 1 What US team did he play for?
   2 How many teams did he play for?

5 1 *How long was it?*
   2 How heavy was it?
   3 How tall was it?
   4 How long were its teeth?

6 1 *What languages does he speak?*
   How many languages does he speak?
   2 What books do you read?/What books do you like reading?
   3 How many pets have you got?
   What pets have you got?
   4 What car does she drive?
   5 How many children have they got?

7 Answers will vary.

Puzzle
Because the little boy is short – he cannot reach the button for the tenth floor.

1 1 *What's he going to do?*
   He's going to jump in the pool.
   2 What's she going to do?
   She's going to paint a picture.
   3 What are they going to do?
   They're going to play basketball.
   4 What's he going to do?
   He's going to take a photo.
   5 What's it going to do?
   It's going to eat the fish.

2 1 *Is* Sue *going to cook* the sausages and chicken?
   2 Is James going to make the sandwiches?
   3 Are Paulo and Carlos going to telephone our friends?
   4 Am I going to tidy the house?

3 1 *No, she isn't. She's going to make a cake.*
   2 No, he isn't. He's going to cook the sausages and chicken.
   3 No, they aren't. They're going to make the sandwiches.
   4 No, you aren't. You're going to telephone our friends.

4
carried	hated	ran
climbed	had	stayed
closed	invented	stopped
came	knew	studied
did	liked	thought
went	made	walked

5 1 *weren't*
   2 dropped
   3 broke
   4 wasn't
   5 was
   6 threw
   7 ran
   8 ate
   9 rained
   10 went
   11 watched
   12 was
   13 didn't have
   14 are going to go

6 1 Where is it from? / Where does it live?
   2 What (food) does it eat?
   3 How big is it?
   4 What colour is it?
   5 How many legs has it got?